Graphing Investigations

TEACHER'S GUIDE
Grade 2

Harcourt

Orlando Austin Chicago New York Toronto London San Diego

Visit *The Learning Site!*
www.harcourtschool.com

Copyright © by Harcourt, Inc.

All rights reserved. No part of this publication may be reproduced or transmitted in any form or by any means, electronic or mechanical, including photocopy, recording, or any information storage and retrieval system, without permission in writing from the publisher.

Permission is hereby granted to individual teachers using the corresponding student's textbook or kit as the major vehicle for regular classroom instruction to photocopy Copying Masters from this publication in classroom quantities for instructional use and not for resale. Requests for information on other matters regarding duplication of this work should be addressed to School Permissions and Copyrights, Harcourt, Inc., 6277 Sea Harbor Drive, Orlando, Florida 32887-6777. Fax: 407-345-2418.

HARCOURT and the Harcourt Logo are trademarks of Harcourt, Inc., registered in the United States of America and/or other jurisdictions.

Printed in the United States of America

ISBN 0-15-337512-4

2 3 4 5 6 7 8 9 10   527   10 09 08 07 06 05 04

Contents

Introduction iv

Week 1 Cupfuls
Use with Chapter 1 1

Week 2 Odds and Evens
Use with Chapter 2 2

Week 3 Story Lengths
Use with Chapter 3 3

Week 4 Birthday Months
Use with Chapter 4 4

Week 5 Doubles and Triples
Use with Chapter 5 5

Week 6 Juice Favorites
Use with Chapter 6 6

Week 7 Phone Number Sums
Use with Chapter 7 7

Week 8 Nifty Fifty
Use with Chapter 8 8

Week 9 Favorite Toys
Use with Chapter 9 9

Week 10 Animal Favorites
Use with Chapter 10 10

Week 11 Thirty-Second Fill
Use with Chapter 11 11

Week 12 Break the Bank
Use with Chapter 12 12

Week 13 Weigh and Pay
Use with Chapter 13 13

Week 14 Rise and Shine
Use with Chapter 14 14

Week 15 Birthdays by the Month
Use with Chapter 15 15

Week 16 Team Scores
Use with Chapter 16 16

Week 17 Toss to Tell
Use with Chapter 17 17

Week 18 Shape Search
Use with Chapter 18 18

Week 19 Tall Towers
Use with Chapter 19 19

Week 20 Folding Facts
Use with Chapter 20 20

Week 21 What Are We Wearing?
Use with Chapter 21 21

Week 22 How Far, How Long, How Wide?
Use with Chapter 22 22

Week 23 Fill to the Brim
Use with Chapter 23 23

Week 24 Tracking High Temperatures
Use with Chapter 24 24

Week 25 Square Cover
Use with Chapter 25 25

Week 26 Pizza Please
Use with Chapter 26 26

Week 27 Dinosaur Dimensions
Use with Chapter 27 27

Week 28 How Much is 1,000?
Use with Chapter 28 28

Week 29 Letters in the Sentence
Use with Chapter 29 29

Week 30 A Week of Walks
Use with Chapter 30 30

Organizer Masters
   sorting, counting, and recording 31
   data collecting and graphing 32

Introduction

Graphing Investigations is a collection of open-ended activities that link to the chapters in *Harcourt Math.* The investigations involve children in predicting, data collecting, graphing, and exploring relationships and trends.

Each investigation opens with "Investigate," which poses a problem and launches the investigation. Nearby is a sample of a completed graph. Your class's graph may differ from the pictured graph due to your unique data and the type of graph your children choose to display the data.

Teaching suggestions supply ideas for guiding children through the investigation. "Content Connections" provides sample questions to show how you might connect graphed data to current math topics.

SUGGESTIONS FOR USING GRAPHING INVESTIGATIONS

Each investigation corresponds to a chapter in *Harcourt Math*'s pupil edition. For example, the Week 4 investigation corresponds to Chapter 4 in the program.

Each investigation takes about a week to complete, but you may shorten or extend an investigation depending on your schedule and children's interests.

- For a longer-term investigation, expand on a topic or follow up on interesting questions that arise during discussions. For example, you might use a child's what-if question as an invitation for further research.

- For a shorter-term investigation, combine several tasks in one session.

- For a weeklong investigation, begin when you start teaching the corresponding chapter in *Harcourt Math*, and wrap up when you complete the chapter.

Use the following plan as a general guide for a weeklong investigation, but expect variations due to the nature of the investigation, for example, whether children collect data in one day or over several days.

The First Day

Discuss the Investigate question(s). You may want to alter the focus of the investigation if the discussion leads to a related topic that sparks children's interest.

Have children define what they hope to achieve in the graphing investigation and what type of data they will need to collect.

Once your class has a clear goal in mind, have children predict the results of the investigation. Record their predictions, and give them an opportunity each day to revise their predictions.

Starting on the first day and continuing throughout the investigation, keep a list of interesting questions that arise from discussions:

- What if . . . ?
- What causes . . . ?
- Is this always true . . . ?

These questions will enrich the investigation, stimulate thinking, and provide interesting topics for customizing or extending the investigation.

The Second Day

Have children make a plan for collecting and organizing the data. For example, children may decide to conduct a survey and make a tally table or to sort shapes or measurements in a diagram.

Although children will not be graphing for another two days, they might think about what type of graph would best achieve their goals. They can then collect and organize their data with the graph in mind to make it easier to later transfer the data to a graph.

Once children have decided on a plan, they can prepare the materials they need to gather the data. For example, they might write and edit their survey question(s) and prepare a table for recording and organizing the data.

The Third Day

Let children gather and organize their data to prepare for graphing on the next day. If children are able to answer the Investigate question(s) using the pre-graphed data, allow them to do so. The next day, after children graph the data, they can revisit the question(s) and discover relationships that might not be apparent in a list, table, or other type of organizer.

The Fourth Day

Have children make the graph. Begin by involving them in determining the graph's title and labels, and when appropriate, the scale. Then you might have volunteers take turns placing data in the classroom graph's pockets.

When children have completed the graph, reread the Investigate question(s) and have them use the graph to find the answer(s).

On either this day or the next, ask questions similar to the Content Connections sample questions to connect chapter content to graph interpretation. Then challenge children to formulate additional questions about the graph.

The Fifth Day

Evaluate and, if appropriate, extend the investigation. You might

- have children write about how the results compared to the predictions: Were children surprised by the results? Do they think the results would differ if they collected more data?

- elicit ideas for ways children could have improved the investigation. Would a different type of graph have worked better? Would a different wording of the survey question have brought different results?

- talk about the interesting questions that arose during the week. Can you use the graph to answer the questions? If not, what kinds of information would you need to gather to answer the questions? Where and how would you gather the information? Use children's responses as a natural and motivating segue into an extension. If your class shows an interest in more than one topic, consider grouping children by their interests for a differentiated approach.

Let *Graphing Investigations* be your guide to classroom adventure. When you can, draw on the uniqueness of your environment and the diversity of children's interests for delightful twists along the way.

Week 1: Cupfuls

INVESTIGATE How many paper clips do you think it takes to fill a cup? How many beans or cubes or buttons do you think it takes to fill a cup?

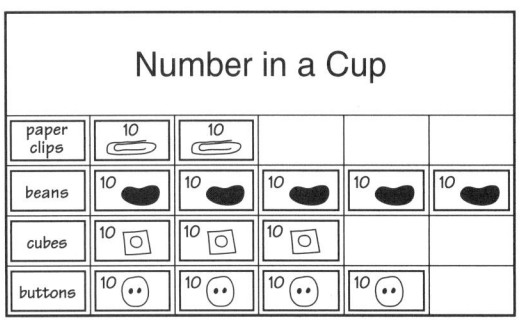

Discuss and Predict

Have children brainstorm a list of small objects to fill a cup with, such as paper clips, beans, buttons, beads, and counters. Help them narrow the list to three or four items. Invite children to predict about how many of each object will fill a cup.

Collect and Organize Data

Help children decide how they will collect and organize data: Will you count each object as you put it into the cup or will you fill the cup and then count the objects? Will you count by one's, two's, five's, or ten's? Will you recount the objects to check the number? Will you record the data in a table or as a list? Will you write numbers or tally marks?

Make and Interpret the Graph

After children have recorded their data, elicit ideas for ways they can show the data in the graph. Because the numbers of objects will be greater than the number of pockets, each graph card will need to represent more than one object.

Have volunteers take turns placing cards in the pocket graph. (The backs of discarded business cards make great pocket graph cards.)

After the graph is complete, ask: How many of each kind of object did it take to fill a cup? Were your predictions close?

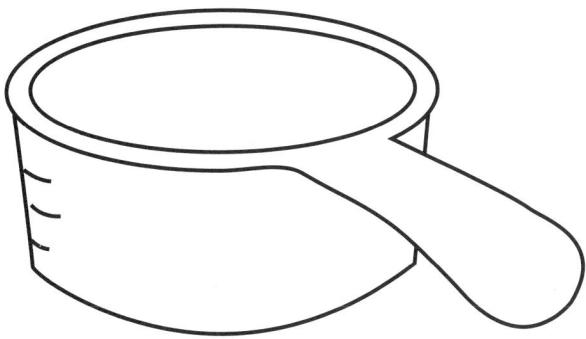

Content Connections

Place Value

Which is greater, the number of beans or the number of buttons?

If each card stood for five objects, how would the graph change?

Graphing Investigations **GI1**

Week 2: Odds and Evens

INVESTIGATE Is there an odd number or an even number of children in our class? Is there an even or odd number of windows in our classroom? Think of other groups of objects in our classroom. Do more groups have an even number of objects? Or do more groups have an odd number of objects?

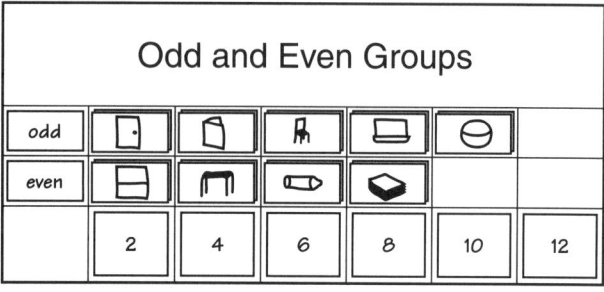

DISCUSS AND PREDICT

Help children brainstorm a list of groups, such as chairs, chair legs, books, windows, bookcases, lights, and tables. Once the list is complete, have children predict whether more groups contain an even or an odd number of objects.

COLLECT AND ORGANIZE DATA

Help children decide how they will gather the data: Will you work in teams? If so, how will you divide up the list? Will one person count and the other tally the items you find?

Help children decide how they will organize the class's data. You might suggest that team members draw pictures on pocket graph cards to represent the groups. On the back of the cards, you might have children write the numbers of objects in the groups. The cards can later be used to make the graph.

MAKE AND INTERPRET THE GRAPH

Guide children in graphing the data: What labels will you need? What will the title be? Then have team members place their pocket graph cards in the graph. After the graph is complete, ask: Did you find more groups that have an odd number of objects, or more groups that have an even number of objects? Is this what you predicted?

Content Connections

ODD AND EVEN NUMBERS

How many odd-numbered groups did you show in the graph?

How many groups of even numbers did you show in the graph?

GI2   Graphing Investigations

Week 3: Story Lengths

INVESTIGATE Sometimes a long story can tell many exciting adventures. Sometimes a short story can tell a good tale in a few words. Do you think children in our class prefer long stories or short stories or a length that is in-between? How can you find out?

Favorite Story Lengths

	1	2	3	4	5	6	7	8
long 20–29	■	■	■	■	■	■	■	
in-between 10–19	■	■	■	■	■	■	■	■
short 0–9	■	■	■	■	■			

Discuss and Predict

Help children define a long story, a short story, and one that is in-between. Children might list their favorite long, short, and in-between stories from memory or by browsing through the class or school library. Once children feel comfortable with their lists, encourage them to further define their groups with page number spans.

Have children predict which length of story their classmates like best.

Collect and Organize Data

Have children suggest ways to gather and organize the data. Children might take a survey, or they might vote by a show of hands or by placing graph cards in boxes labeled *long*, *short*, and *in-between*. They might organize the data as tallies, numbers, or as grouped cards.

Make and Interpret the Graph

Guide children in choosing the graph title and labels. Then have children place their pocket graph cards in the graph. After children complete the graph, ask: What length of story do most children in our class like the best? Is this what you predicted?

Content Connections

ORDINAL AND ORDER
What are the first, second, and third favorite story lengths?

Graphing Investigations **GI3**

Week 4: Birthday Months

INVESTIGATE In which month is your birthday? In which month does our class have the most birthdays?

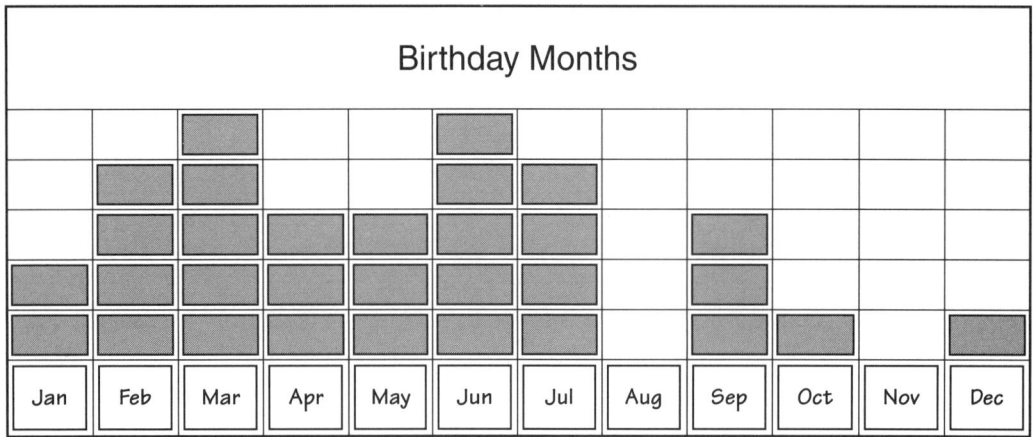

DISCUSS AND PREDICT

Some children might know each other's birthdays from attending birthday parties or from being friends. Ask children to predict which month has the greatest number of their classmate's birthdays.

COLLECT AND ORGANIZE DATA

Have children decide what kind of information they need to collect to determine the accuracy of their predictions: How will you find out in which months your classmates were born? Does it matter what day of the month the birthday is on?

Display a month-by-month calendar and point out how the months are shown in order from January to December for the whole year. Ask each child to tell the class when his or her birthday is. Record children's responses by writing each child's name in the calendar on his or her birthday. Note if any children share the same birth date.

After all children have responded, have them decide how they will organize the birthday information. For example, children might tally the birthdays by month and later represent the tallies as cards in the graph. Or they might choose to each take a card, and then take turns placing their cards in the graph as you or a volunteer announces each month.

MAKE AND INTERPRET THE GRAPH

Guide children in deciding how they can graph the data: How can you use the pocket graph? What labels will you put across the bottom? What will the title be? After the graph is complete, ask: In which month do the greatest number of you have a birthday? Is this what you predicted?

USE A GRAPH

Which month has the fewest birthdays?

Does any month have no birthdays?

Do any months have the same number of birthdays? How can you tell?

Week 5: Doubles and Triples

INVESTIGATE If you tossed three number cubes, do you think any of the three numbers would be the same? Suppose you tossed the three cubes 24 times, which would you get most often, a double or a triple or neither?

Discuss and Predict
Remind children that each cube is numbered 1–6. Ask them to name the six possible doubles, the six possible triples, and two or three combinations that are neither doubles or triples. Then have children predict which they will toss most often, doubles, triples, or neither.

Collect and Organize Data
Have children decide how they want to collect and record the data: Will volunteers take turns rolling the cubes or will four groups each roll the cubes six times? Will you make a tally table or use a different kind of organizer to record the outcomes?

If children work in groups, you might suggest that they use the floor as a surface to avoid having cubes roll off their desks. Afterwards, help them to organize the groups' data into a class table.

Make and Interpret the Graph
Guide children in graphing their data: What kind of graph will you make? What labels and numbers will you use? What will you title the graph?

After the graph is finished ask: Which did you toss more often, doubles, triples, or neither? Is this what you predicted?

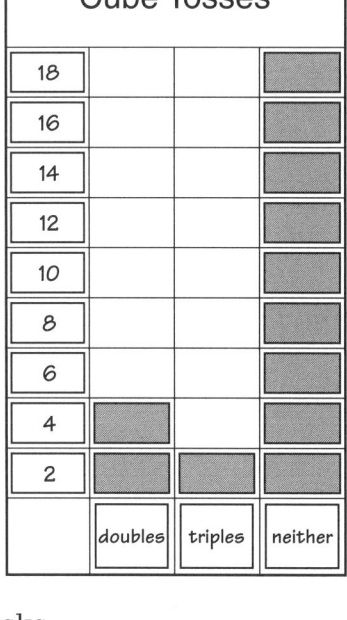

Content Connections

ADDITION STRATEGIES
What are all the sums you can get from tossing a double on two cubes?

What are all the sums you can get from tossing a triple on three cubes?

Graphing Investigations **GI5**

Week 6: Juice Favorites

INVESTIGATE What is your favorite kind of juice? What do you think is the favorite juice among the children in our classroom?

Discuss and Predict

Have children brainstorm a list of their favorite juices. Write the list on the board for later reference. Then have children predict which of the juices will be the class favorite.

Have children discuss how they will collect and organize the data: Will you vote by a show of hands? Will you write your favorites on cards and then sort the cards by type of juice? How will you keep track of the number of choices? Will you organize the cards into groups or make a table using tallies or numbers or both? What will you do if someone says they have two favorite juices? Will you count both or have the person select one?

Collect and Organize Data

Have children begin collecting the data based on the decisions they made. Allow adjustments if it improves the process.

Make and Interpret the Graph

Guide children in using the pocket graph to graph the data: How many labels will you include? What numbers will you use? What will the title be? After children complete the graph, ask: What is the favorite juice in our class? Is this the juice you predicted?

Our Favorite Juices

	orange	apple	grape	berry	melon
6	■				
5	■	■			
4	■	■		■	
3	■	■	■	■	
2	■	■	■	■	■
1	■	■	■	■	■

Content Connections

Subtraction

What is the difference between the number of children who chose the two most favorite juices and the number of children who chose the least two favorite juices?

Phone Number Sums

INVESTIGATE Phone numbers end in 4 digits. Suppose each person in class chose 4 digits by pointing at listings in the yellow pages with their eyes shut. Then suppose children used their 4 digits to make 2 two-digit numbers. If everyone tried to arrange the digits to make the greatest sum, what sum would most children get?

DISCUSS AND PREDICT

Model the process of determining the greatest two-digit numbers from the last 4 digits of a telephone number. You may wish to use the school's phone number for this purpose. Encourage children to discuss how they can find the greatest sums: How can you use place value to determine whether 26 or 62 is the greater number? Do you have to make the greatest possible two-digit numbers to get the greatest possible sum? Explain. Then ask children to estimate what sum most children will get. Allow children to give ranges as well as specific numbers.

COLLECT AND ORGANIZE DATA

Have children discuss how they want to collect their data: How will you keep track of everyone's sums? Will you list them on the board in order from least to greatest? Will you group the sums in categories, such as sums from 0 to 49, from 50 to 99, and so forth? If children select ranges, allow them to revise their predictions based on the ranges.

MAKE AND INTERPRET THE GRAPH

Help children use their data to construct a pocket graph. For labels, they might think about the categories they gave to their organized data. Once children have completed the graph, have them check their predictions against the graph. Encourage them to infer reasons why their predictions were alike or different from the graphed results.

Our Greatest Sums

	0–49	50–99	100–149	150–199
18		■		
16		■		
14		■		
12		■		
10		■		
8		■	■	
6		■	■	
4	■	■	■	
2	■	■	■	■

Content Connections

TWO-DIGIT ADDITION

How many children had sums that were less than 100?

How many children had sums that were greater than 100?

Week 8: Nifty Fifty

INVESTIGATE Suppose you had 2 bags, each containing the digits 0–9. You took 2 digits from the first bag and placed them side by side in the order that you took them. You did the same with the other bag. Having made 2 two-digit numbers, you added them. Was your sum less than 50, exactly 50, or greater than 50?

Discuss and Predict

Have children help you make two sets of number cards, numbered 0–9. Each set of cards should be a different color and kept in a separate paper bag.

Have a volunteer demonstrate the scenario set up in "Investigate." Before the child adds the numbers, have the class estimate whether the sum is less than 50, exactly 50, or greater than 50. After the child adds to check, invite children to predict which estimate would occur most often if they were to repeat the experiment 12 times.

Collect and Organize Data

Have children decide how to tally the sums into three categories—less than 50, exactly 50, and greater than 50. Suggest that children take turns taking cards and writing the addends on the board. Each time have the class estimate whether the sum is less than 50, exactly 50, or greater than 50. Then call on a volunteer to find the sum to confirm the estimate. Be sure to replace all cards in their respective bags before the next child takes a turn.

Make and Interpret the Graph

Have children decide how to graph their estimates: What type of graph will you use? What labels will the graph need? How will you number the pockets? Then have children transfer their data to the graph. When the graph is complete, have children review their predictions: Which estimate occurs most often, less than 50, exactly 50 or greater than 50?

Content Connections

Two-Digit Addition
Were any of the sums equal to 50?
How did you estimate what the sum of the two-digit numbers would be?
What is the greatest sum you could make? The least sum?

GI8 Graphing Investigations

Week 9 — Favorite Toys

INVESTIGATE Do you have a favorite toy? What do you think is your classmates' favorite toy and your classmates' second favorite toy?

DISCUSS AND PREDICT

Engage children in a discussion of their favorite toys. Make a list of the toys on the board. Then help children narrow the list to five or six items by putting like toys into groups. For example, all dolls could go into one group. All toy cars could go into another group. Then ask children to predict which toys on the list will be the class favorite and second favorite.

COLLECT AND ORGANIZE DATA

Have children decide how they want to collect the data: Will you conduct a survey? Will you have each child place a tally mark next to the name of his or her favorite toy on the board? Will children write the names of their favorite toys on cards that you can sort and count? Will children vote by raising their hands? Then guide children as they begin collecting and organizing their data.

MAKE AND INTERPRET THE GRAPH

Guide children in making labels for the graph. You may wish to suggest that each category be illustrated with a picture on a pocket graph card. Ask: Where will you place the labels for the toys? What numbers will you place in the graph? What title will the graph have? After children complete the graph, have them compare the results shown on the graph with their predictions: What is the favorite toy in our class? What is the second most favorite? Are these the toys you predicted?

Content Connections

SUBTRACTION

Twenty-one children chose their favorites. How many children did *not* choose trains as their favorite?

How many more children chose cars than chose teddy bears?

Graphing Investigations

Week 10: Animal Favorites

INVESTIGATE Have you ever been to a zoo or seen one on television? How many different kinds of animals did you see? Which animal was your favorite? Which do you think is our class's favorite animal? Our second favorite?

Zoo Animal Favorites

Animal				
Panda	■	■	■	■
Tiger	■	■	■	
Elephant	■	■	■	
Giraffe	■	■		
Kangaroo	■	■		
Lion	■			
Monkey	■	■		
Parrot	■			
	2	4	6	8

Discuss and Predict

As children talk about their favorite animals, make a list of the animals they identify. If the list is long, help children narrow it down to seven or eight choices by grouping similar animals. For example, different kinds of bears could all be placed in one category.

Then ask: Which animal do you think will be the class favorite? The second most favorite? Have children record their predictions for later.

Collect and Organize Data

Ask children how they can use the list to find the favorite animal for the class: Will you have everyone place tally marks next to their favorite animals on the list? Will you have children vote for their favorites with graph cards? Will you allow children to choose more than one favorite animal?

Have each child choose a favorite animal by recording a tally mark on the list or by voting with a card.

Make and Interpret the Graph

Guide children in making labels for a pocket graph. They may want to draw a picture on a card of each animal on the list, and then use the pictures as labels for the graph. Ask: Will you put the labels along the bottom of the graph or along the side? What numbers will you put on the graph? Where will you put them? Once the graph is completed, have children compare the results: Which is our class's favorite animal? Which is the second most favorite? Is this what you predicted?

Content Connections

ADDITION AND SUBTRACTION

How many children chose the three least favorite animals?

How many more children chose animals with 4 legs than animals with 2 legs?

Week 11: Thirty-Second Fill

INVESTIGATE About how many paper clips do you think you or a classmate can put into a paper cup in thirty seconds?

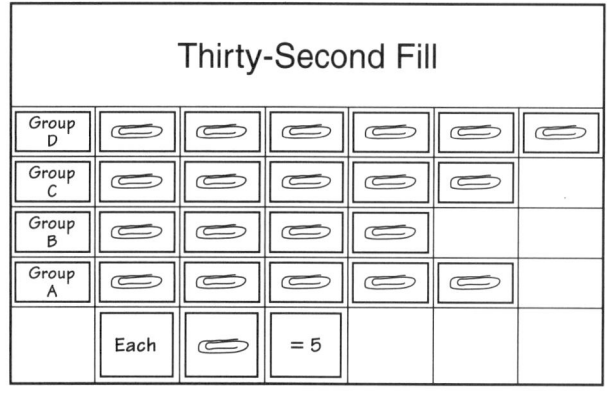

Discuss and Predict

If you have a classroom clock with a second hand or several timers, you might suggest that children work in groups so that they can take turns being the timer and the filler. If not, you might keep the time while children fill their cups.

Help children define the investigation: Will you put one or more than one paper clip in your cup at a time? Will you begin with practice trials? Will you report your group's best score or each child's score?

Then have children predict about how many paper clips they will be able to put in their cups based on their agreed-to rules. Give children an opportunity to explain their thinking. For example, children might reason that if they can move one paper clip each second, then they should be able to move thirty paper clips in thirty seconds.

Collect and Organize Data

Have children decide how they will collect and organize their data. They might contribute to a class list and then order their numbers from least to greatest to examine the range.

Make and Interpret the Graph

Guide children in deciding how to graph their data. If the number of paper clips exceeds the number of pockets, then children need to decide on a value greater than one for a pictograph symbol or on an interval greater than one for a bar graph scale.

After children have completed the graph, ask: About how many paper clips can you put into a paper cup in 30 seconds? How does that compare to your predictions?

Content Connections

Addition and Subtraction

What is the difference between the greatest number of paper clips and the least number?

If you were allowed twice as much time to complete the activity, how many paper clips do you think you could put into the cup?

Graphing Investigations   GI11

Week 12: Break the Bank

INVESTIGATE After saving for ages, you have filled an old sugar bowl with an equal number of pennies, nickels, dimes, and quarters. To keep from spending all of your money at once, you decide to stir up the coins and scoop out a spoonful each week for spending. About how much money do you get in one spoonful? Is this true for other spoonfuls?

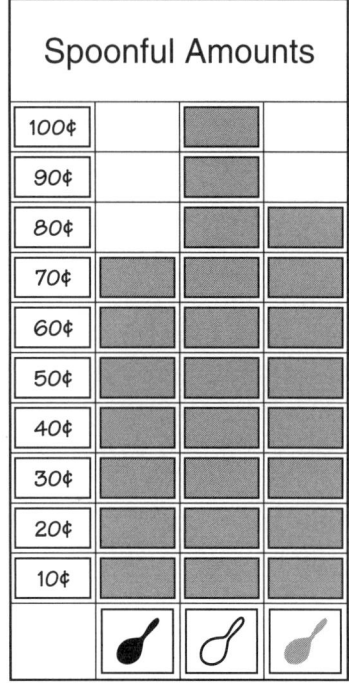

Discuss and Predict

Have children help you take an inventory of your class's play money. Challenge them to fill as many sugar bowls or other containers they can fill with coins based on the "Investigate" scenario.

Let children examine the spoons for scooping. Then have them estimate the amount of money that they will get in one spoonful and whether that is true for other spoonfuls.

Collect and Organize Data

You might suggest that children work in groups, one group for each "sugar bowl." Then help them plan how they will achieve their goals: How many times will you need to scoop to check your estimates? Will you return coins to the sugar bowl between scoops, or keep scooping until you run out of coins? Will your spoonfuls be rounded or level?

Once children have recorded their data, let them discuss their findings and write their amounts on the board.

Make and Interpret the Graph

Point out that by graphing the amounts, children can visually compare each of their amounts to other amounts. Once they have finished the graph, ask: About how much money do you get in one spoonful? Is this true for other spoonfuls?

Content Connections

MONEY
What was the greatest amount? What was the least value of coins scooped? What was the difference between the two?

What is the sum for all the coins scooped up?

Week 13: Weigh and Pay

INVESTIGATE How much does a dollar's worth of pennies weigh? A dollar's worth of nickels? A dollar's worth of dimes? A dollar's worth of quarters? How do the weights compare?

Discuss and Predict

Talk about how many of each type of coin are equivalent to one dollar: 100 pennies, 20 nickels, 10 dimes, 4 quarters. Have children take turns handling one of each coin. Then invite them to estimate the weight of each dollar's worth and to talk about how their estimates compare.

Collect and Organize Data

Show children a balance or spring scale. The type of scale you have may determine whether children measure in ounces, grams, or in nonstandard units. If there is a choice of units, children might measure a handful of coins to judge that smaller units, ounces or grams, world work better than larger units, pounds or kilograms.

Children might enjoy weighing one group of coins each day. After children weigh a group of coins, they can use their findings to revise their estimates for the weight of the next day's coins.

Make and Interpret the Graph

Help children decide on a type of graph. If you decide on a bar graph, you may want to address two different meanings of *scale*: a measurement tool, the graph's numbers.

When children have completed the graph, have them compare their estimates to the graphed data. Talk about which they would rather carry in their pockets—a dollar's worth of pennies, nickels, dimes, or quarters.

Weights of Dollars (in Ounces)

8	■		
7	■		
6	■		
5	■	■	
4	■	■	
3	■	■	
2	■	■	
1	■	■	■	■
	$1.00 in pennies	$1.00 in nickels	$1.00 in dimes	$1.00 in quarters

Content Connections

MONEY
There are 16 ounces in 1 pound. About how much would 1 pound of pennies be worth?

How much do all of the pennies and nickels weigh altogether?

Week 14 Rise and Shine

INVESTIGATE Sunrise times change during the year. How much does the sunrise time change from day to day where you live? Is it getting lighter earlier or later each day?

Discuss and Predict

Invite children to share what they know about the time the sun rises. Some may recall whether it was lighter or dark outside when they woke up, ate breakfast, or left for school.

Explain that the sunrise may appear to occur at the same time every morning because the time difference from day to day is gradual. A good source for finding sunrise times is the local paper. Have children predict how the sunrise times will change each day during the week.

Collect and Organize Data

For four or five days help children locate the times of sunrise in the newspaper. Record the information on the board or on chart paper. Each day, have children compare the sunrise time to those of the preceding day(s). Invite children to predict tomorrow's sunrise time.

Make and Interpret the Graph

Have children make and insert graph labels. Then invite volunteers to place cards in the graph to show the times. Referring to the completed graph, have children look for patterns: About how many minutes' difference is there each day? Does the sun rise earlier or later each day? Is this what you predicted?

Sunrise Times

	Mon	Tues	Wed	Thur
6:07				
6:06				▨
6:05				▨
6:04			▨	▨
6:03		▨	▨	▨
6:02		▨	▨	▨
6:01	▨	▨	▨	▨

Content Connections

TIME

What is the difference between the time the sun rose on Tuesday and the time it rose on Wednesday?

Could you use a graph like this to show what time the sun sets? What do you think such a graph would show?

Graphing Investigations

Week 15: Birthdays by the Month

INVESTIGATE Does our class have more birthdays before the middle of a month or after the middle of the month?

DISCUSS AND PREDICT

Remind children that there are twenty-eight to thirty-one days in a month. Then have them determine the middle of each month. For a 31-day month they might choose the 16th because an equal number of days precede and follow the 16th. However, children would need to decide whether to count birthdays falling on the 16th as occurring in the first or last half of a month.

Then have children predict whether they have more birthdays before or after the middle of each month.

COLLECT AND ORGANIZE DATA

Help children decide how they will collect the data they need about their classmates' birthdays. One possibility is to make a month-by-month tally table on the board having the categories *before* and *after*. As a volunteer displays a month on the calendar, children tally in which half of that month their birthdays occur.

MAKE AND INTERPRET THE GRAPH

Guide children in transferring their data to the graph. When the graph is complete, have children visually compare the numbers of birthdays in the two parts of the months. Then have them check their findings against their predictions.

Content Connections

CALENDAR

How many birthdays occur in the first parts of months?

How many more birthdays occur in the first parts of the months than in the last parts of months?

Team Scores

INVESTIGATE Most games have a winner. Often the winner is the team or person with the most points by the end of the game. If you play a game with number cubes, how can you find which team is the winner? Which team has the most points?

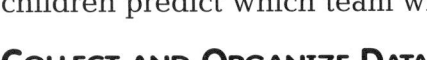

DISCUSS AND PREDICT

Help children explore games in which they have used scoring sheets to keep track of points: What information do you keep on the scoring sheet? How does it show which person or team is winning? How does keeping score help you determine the winner?

Have children work together to make up their own game using number cubes. For example, they might decide to play a game where each team in turn tosses three number cubes and adds the numbers. The team with the greatest sum gets 1 point. If the team sums are equal, both teams get 1 point. If a team has the wrong sum, it loses 1 point. The team with the most points after ten rounds wins.

After a game has been decided on, have children plan their scoring sheets: Do you need to show the names of the teams or the names of the players on the sheet? How will you show your scoring method? What other information might you include? Then have children predict which team will have the highest score.

COLLECT AND ORGANIZE DATA

Have children discuss how they want to collect the data for a graph: Does each team have a scoring sheet with its score total on it? Will each team record its score on the board next to the team's name? Will you have each team turn in its score on a slip of paper and then list the scores?

MAKE AND INTERPRET THE GRAPH

Have children decide how to construct a graph to show their data. After the graph is completed, have children compare team scores. Ask: Which team or teams have the highest score? Was this about what you predicted?

Content Connections

GRAPHS AND TABLES

What two teams had the same scores?

What was the difference between the highest score and the lowest score?

What is another way you could have displayed this data?

GI16   Graphing Investigations

Toss to Tell

INVESTIGATE If you tossed three coins would you be most likely to get all heads, all tails, or a mixture of both?

Three-Coin Toss

heads	▨	▨						
tails	▨	▨						
both	▨	▨	▨	▨	▨	▨	▨	▨
	5	10	15	20	25	30	35	40

Discuss and Predict

Place three coins on a table. Have a volunteer turn over the coins as necessary to show three heads and then three tails. Then have several children take turns showing other combinations, such as HTT, HTH, HHT, and so on.

Help children decide on a number of trials. If they suggest as many as 100, then they might work in groups and combine results.

Have children predict the results.

Collect and Organize Data

If children work in groups, then each group might keep its own tally table. Later, group members can contribute to a class table.

You might suggest that children toss their coins onto a paper towel or carpet so the coins will not roll when they land.

Make and Interpret the Graph

Help children use the class's totals to decide on a bar-graph scale or on a value for a pictograph symbol.

When children have finished the graph they may be surprised by how many "mixed" tosses they have. If children are interested, you might show them that while there is one combination for all heads, one for all tails, there are six combinations (HTT, HHT, HTH, THH, THT, TTH) for a mixture.

Content Connections

PROBABILITY

What do you predict the number of heads would be if you made twice as many tosses?

Graphing Investigations

Week 18: Shape Search

INVESTIGATE What is the shape of the top step of a sliding board? What is the shape of a basketball hoop? What is the shape of a swing seat? What shape do you think you could find most often on a playground?

Playground Shapes

rhombus									
trapezoid	▓	▓							
circle	▓	▓	▓						
triangle	▓								
rectangle	▓	▓	▓	▓	▓	▓	▓	▓	▓
square	▓	▓	▓	▓	▓	▓	▓		
	2	4	6	8	10	12	14	16	18

Discuss and Predict

Engage children in a discussion of their favorite playground equipment. As the discussion progresses, focus their attention on the shapes they might see. Ask: Where might you find triangles on the playground? Where might you find rectangles? What kind of shapes do you think you could find on the things made for climbing? Are there any shapes drawn on the ground for playing games? If you did a "shape search," which shape would you predict you would find most often?

Collect and Organize Data

Guide children as they plan a "shape search" survey of the playground. If they work in groups, they might record the name of the object on which they found each shape to avoid duplication when they combine results.

Help them make a survey sheet: What shapes will you include in your survey? How do you want to list them on your survey sheet? Then model the survey sheet by looking at and discussing objects in the classroom.

Observe children as they collect their data on the playground. When the surveys are complete, bring children back to the classroom and tally the groups' results on the board.

Make and Interpret the Graph

Have children discuss how they will graph the data they have collected: What type of graph will you use? What labels should it have? Where will these labels go? What would make a good title for the graph? Once children have completed the graph, have them compare the numbers of different shapes they found. Ask: Which shape did you find the most of? Is this the shape you predicted?

Content Connections

Plane Shapes

How many more rectangles than squares did you find?

How many four-sided shapes did you find?

Tall Towers

INVESTIGATE Have you ever stacked connecting cubes one on top of the other to make a tall tower? How many cubes do you think you can stack before your tower falls over? How many cubes do you think would be in our class's tallest tower?

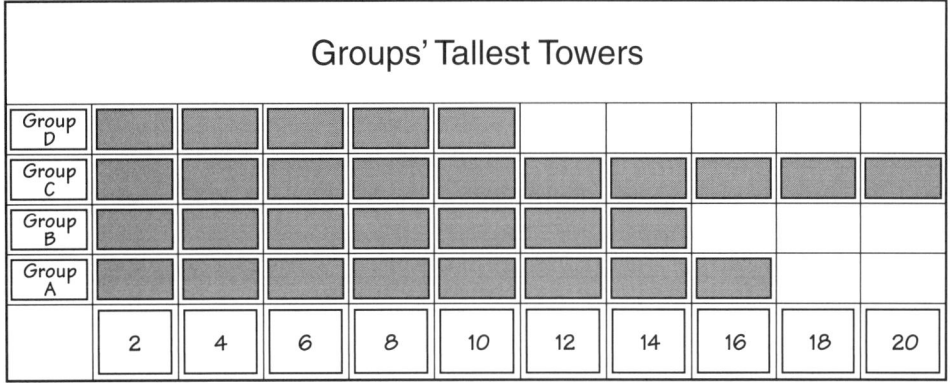

DISCUSS AND PREDICT

You may want to group children so they can share materials and take turns building towers. Guide children to define the investigation by discussing how many towers each child will build. Then children might compare the number of cubes they used to determine who built the tallest tower in each group, and then in the class.

Have children estimate how many cubes tall their towers and the tallest tower will be.

COLLECT AND ORGANIZE DATA

Have children discuss how they will keep track of the number of cubes they use: Will you count cubes as you stack them? Will you count all the cubes in the tower after it falls down? Will you write the number of cubes you used on a piece of paper?

Talk about ways in which children can organize groups' data to find the class's tallest tower.

MAKE AND INTERPRET THE GRAPH

Have children decide on a type of graph, and invite volunteers to take turns placing pocket cards.

Discuss whether the graph shows the tallest towers in the class, keeping in mind that this may not always be the case. For example, one group may have built the two tallest towers, but only one of the two might be shown on the graph.

Conclude by having children use the graph to check their predictions.

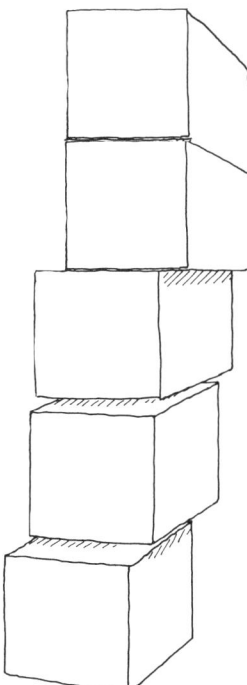

Content Connections

SOLID FIGURES
What shape was your tower when you finished building it?

Why are the building blocks you used to make your tower called cubes?

Folding Facts

INVESTIGATE Are the letters A and B symmetrical? Does it depend on how the letters are written? If you wrote all the uppercase letters as symmetrically as possible, would the alphabet have more symmetrical letters or more letters that are not symmetrical? How can you find out?

DISCUSS AND PREDICT

Display a variety of symmetrical shapes, such as circles, squares, rectangles, triangles, and hearts. Remind children that a square is symmetrical because when you fold it in half, both halves match exactly. Then call on volunteers to identify the fold lines that prove that each of the other shapes is symmetrical.

Place alphabet cards in a container such as a basket or box. Because the cards may get damaged, you may wish to make your own. Then have children discuss how they will decide if each letter has a line of symmetry: Will you work in pairs or individually? Will one person draw a letter and the other look for a fold line to show the letter is symmetrical? How will you keep track of the letters that are symmetrical? Remind children that they are only looking for symmetry in uppercase, capital, letters. Then have them predict if there will be more symmetrical letters or more letters that are not symmetrical.

COLLECT AND ORGANIZE DATA

Help children decide how they will record the data. You may want to suggest that children print the alphabet on the board or on a strip of paper and label each letter "yes" or "no." As another alternative, you may want children to sort the letters and then count the number of cards in each group.

MAKE AND INTERPRET THE GRAPH

Have children decide how they will record their totals on the pocket graph: What labels will you put along the bottom of the graph? What numbers will you put along the side of the graph? What would make a good title for the graph? Then have children check their predictions: Were there more symmetrical letters or more letters that were not symmetrical? How can you tell by looking at the graph?

Is It Symmetrical?		
16	Y	
14	W	
12	T	
10	M	S
8	I	G
6	E	N
4	C	J
2	A	F
	Yes	No

Content Connections

SYMMETRY

How many letters of the alphabet are symmetrical? How many are not symmetrical?

Are any of the letters in your name symmetrical? Which one(s)?

Week 21: What Are We Wearing?

INVESTIGATE Suppose your school wants to have children wear uniforms, but uniforms that children like. The school wants to know what tops children usually wear. Can you help the school by finding out what tops children in your class are wearing?

Discuss and Predict

Have children decide what characteristic of tops they will investigate: Will you find the most common color? the most common print? the most common sleeve length? Once children decide on the category of data they will collect, you may want them to refine the category by identifying specific characteristics, such as what colors, what prints, what types of sleeves.

Have children decide how they will collect and record the data: Will you survey classmates or record your observations? If you use a survey, will you ask what each person is wearing or what they usually like to wear? Then have children predict which characteristic of tops is most common among their classmates.

Colors of Our Tops

red	white	blue	yellow	brown	black
👕	👕	👕	👕		👕
👕	👕	👕	👕		👕
👕	👕	👕	👕		
👕	👕	👕			
👕	👕	👕			
👕		👕			
👕					

Collect and Organize Data

Have children decide how they want to collect their data: Will you use a tally table or make a list? Who will collect and record the data? If children choose to use tallies, check to be sure they are using them correctly.

Make and Interpret the Graph

Help children decide how to present their data using a pocket graph. If children have considered two common characteristics, then they might make two different graphs, one on each side of the pocket graph.

When the graph is complete, ask: What are the most common types of tops in your class? Was your prediction correct?

Content Connections

PATTERNS

How many children chose the most popular color? The least popular color?

What is the difference between the number of choices for the most popular color and the number of choices for the least popular color?

Graphing Investigations **GI21**

Week 22: How Far, How Long, How Wide?

INVESTIGATE Is the door wider than the table? What are some ways you can find out? If you measure both widths with paper clips, how could you tell which is wider? Would you get the same result if you measured with craft sticks? With connecting cubes?

Discuss and Predict

Have children brainstorm some lengths to measure and to compare: Will you measure the width of a desktop? The width of the door? The distance from the floor to the chalkboard? The length of four erasers laid end-to-end? Decide what measurement units to use: Can you use paper clips? Connecting cubes? Craft sticks or some other item?

Before children begin, you may want to model how to measure using nonstandard units. Have one child estimate the number of paper clips needed to find the length of an object. Then have two volunteers place the paper clips end-to-end as the class counts the number used. Then have children predict which objects are longer or wider.

Collect and Organize Data

Display the list of objects to be measured and add one column for estimates and one column for measurements. You may want children to work in teams, so that each team can measure all the objects on the list using one type of unit. Review with children how to collect and record their data.

Make and Interpret the Graph

Have children decide how to graph the data. To make comparisons, they might compare the lengths of objects using one measurement unit, or they might make two graphs as shown.

Have children check their estimates: Which object is wider (or longer)? Do you get the same result using other measurement units?

Content Connections

MEASUREMENT

Are any of the measurements the same? Why or why not?

Do we usually measure in inches or paper clips? Why?

Week 23: Fill to the Brim

INVESTIGATE I have a cup in my hand. If you have five paper clips, will they fill this cup? Will five crayons fill the cup? Will five lima beans fill the cup? How many of each item will you need to fill the cup to the brim? When you fill the cup with larger items, will you need more or less of them than when you fill it with smaller items?

Discuss and Predict

Have children decide what they will use to fill the cup. Some items children might consider include the following: base-ten units, crayons, links, large paper clips, peanuts, dry lima beans, or popped corn. Then have children estimate which item they will need the most of to fill the cup.

Collect and Organize Data

Have children decide how they will record their data: Will you list the items in a table? Will you first record an estimate of the number of each item needed to fill the cup, and then record the exact number of each item needed to fill the cup?

Make and Interpret the Graph

Help children decide how to graph the data on the pocket graph: What labels will you use? What will the title be? What scale will work best? After children complete the graph, ask: Which item did you need the most of to fill the cup? Is this the largest item? Is it the smallest item? Were your predictions about which item you would need the most of to fill the cup correct?

Number in a Cup

	paper clips	popcorn	bears	cubes
100		■		
90		■		
80	■	■		
70				
60	■	■	■	
50	■	■	■	■
40	■	■	■	■
30	■	■	■	■
20	■	■	■	■
10	■	■	■	■

Content Connections

MEASUREMENT
Would you need more than or fewer than 100 grains of rice to fill the cup? How do you know?

Week 24: Tracking High Temperatures

INVESTIGATE Will the high temperature be the same every day this week? If not, by how many degrees might it vary?

Discuss and Predict

Have children decide how they will find the temperature data they need: Will you use the newspaper to find the high temperature for each day? Will you use the radio or television? Will you use the Internet?

If you find a source with temperature data in degrees Celsius, encourage children to record these data and to relate these temperatures to what the weather is like each day. Suggest that the recording sheet be displayed where all members of the class can examine it. Then have children predict a trend in the highest temperatures.

Collect and Organize Data

Have children decide how they will record their data: Will one child record the temperatures, or will different children record the temperatures? Will you make a table to record the temperatures? Will the table show the days of the week? Will it have places to write the high temperatures? Will you record only temperatures for school days or for an entire week?

Make and Interpret the Graph

Help children decide how to graph the data: Will you label the horizontal axis with five or seven days of the week? How will you label the vertical axis? What will your scale be? When the graph is complete, ask: What was the highest temperature for the week? Is this about what you predicted? By how many degrees did the high temperatures vary during the week? Were you able to predict a trend in temperatures for this time of year?

High Temperatures

	Mon	Tues	Wed	Thurs	Fri
75					▓
74				▓	▓
73	▓			▓	▓
72	▓			▓	▓
71	▓	▓	▓	▓	▓
70	▓	▓	▓	▓	▓

Content Connections

MEASUREMENT

What was the high temperature for Monday?

What was the difference between the high temperatures for each day of the week?

Square Cover

INVESTIGATE About how many connecting cubes would you need to cover a six-inch by six-inch square? Would it take more or fewer self-stick notes to cover the square? More or fewer lima beans?

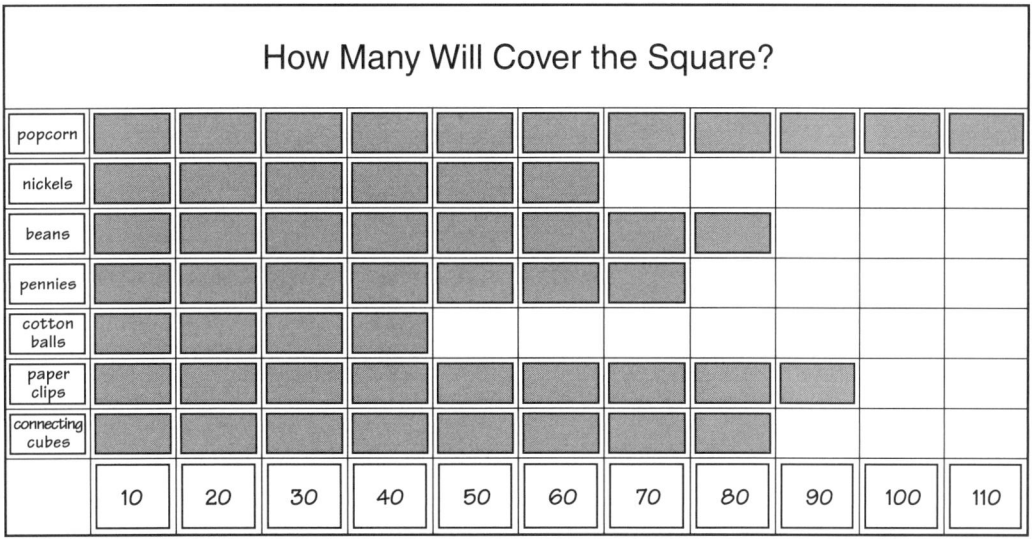

DISCUSS AND PREDICT

You may want to model the covering process by asking a volunteer to cover a six-inch by six-inch square of paper with connecting cubes. Then have the class count in unison as you remove the cubes one by one.

Divide the class into groups. Provide each group with a six-inch by six-inch square. Have children decide which items they will use to cover their squares, for example, links, square tiles, cotton balls, base-ten blocks, dry lima beans, pennies, pattern blocks, nickels, 1-inch cubes, self-stick notes, dry cereal pieces, or dry pasta pieces. Keep a list of their suggestions on the board. When the list is complete, have each group select an item from the list. Then have the children in each group estimate how many of their chosen item will cover their square and whether they would use more or fewer objects than other groups would use.

COLLECT AND ORGANIZE DATA

Have children decide how they will record the data: Will you use a table or will you make a list?

Check to be sure children fit as many items as possible on the square without overlapping.

MAKE AND INTERPRET THE GRAPH

Guide children in graphing their data. After they agree on labels and a scale, group representatives could take turns placing cards in the graph.

After children complete the graph, ask: How did your group's number of objects compare to other groups' number of objects? How does this compare to your estimates?

Content Connections

AREA

What was the greatest number of items needed to cover the square? Why?

Does it take more pennies or more nickels to cover the square? How do you know?

Week 26: Pizza Please

INVESTIGATE There are many different kinds of pizza toppings. What is your favorite topping? What do you think is the favorite pizza topping in our class? Would it be possible for two toppings to tie as the favorite? How can you find out what the favorite topping is?

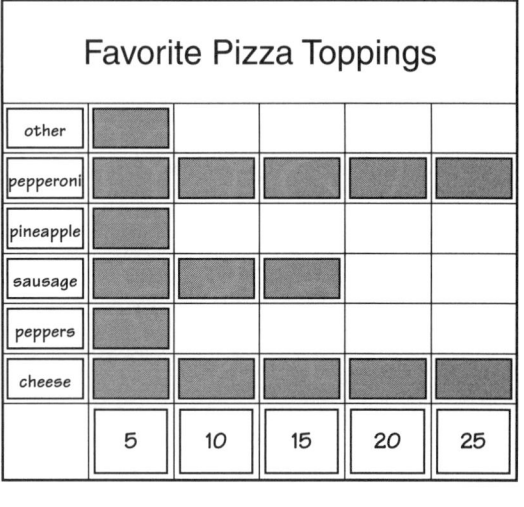

Discuss and Predict

Have children brainstorm a list of all the pizza toppings they have seen or eaten. Write this list on the board as a reminder of the choices and to use as a tally chart later.

You may wish to give each child a small round paper plate or a six-inch circle cut from construction paper to serve as a model of a pizza. Children can fold the plate or circle in half twice to make four "pieces." In each section, suggest that children draw and label a favorite pizza topping. Then have children decide what information from their pizza drawings they will collect: Will you tally every topping each person drew? Will you tally only one topping for each person? Will you use a list or a tally table to keep track? Then have children predict which topping will be the favorite among the class.

Collect and Organize Data

As children record their favorite toppings, remind them of the number of toppings they should record. After the data is recorded, you may want to have volunteers total the tally marks next to each topping listed. If there are too many toppings to graph easily on the pocket graph, you may want to make an "Other" category to include the toppings with the fewest votes.

Make and Interpret the Graph

Help children plan their pocket graph: What numbers will you put along the bottom of the graph? What do these numbers stand for? What labels will you put along the side of the graph? What do these labels stand for? What would make a good title for the graph? After children complete the graph, ask: What is the favorite pizza topping in our class? Is this the topping that you predicted?

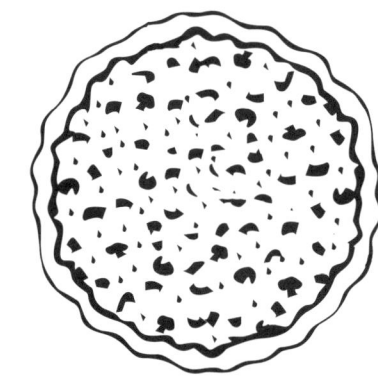

Content Connections

FRACTIONS

What fraction of the pizza does each of your topping choices represent?

If you covered two pieces of your pizza with one topping and two pieces with another topping, what fraction of your pizza would be covered by each one?

GI26 Graphing Investigations

Dinosaur Dimensions

INVESTIGATE Many different kinds of dinosaurs once roamed the Earth. Some were as small as a dog. Others were so big they wouldn't even fit into this room. Which of your favorite dinosaurs do you think could fit into this room?

Length	Dinosaur
3	FABROSAURUS
7	ADSAURUS
7	MINMI
10	DRAVIDSAURUS
10	COLELOPHYSIS
16	MARSHOSAURUS
17	KENTOSAURUS
18	BACTROSAURUS
26	ALBERTOSAURUS
30	HADROSAURUS
42	EDMONTOSAURUS
55	CAMARASAURUS
65	ALAMOSAURUS
70	APATOSAURUS

Discuss and Predict

Have children brainstorm a list of dinosaur names. Some dinosaurs they may be familiar with include brontosaurus, stegosaurus, brachiosaurus, tyrannosaurus, and adasaurus. Once the list is complete, ask children to predict whether any of the dinosaurs on the list could fit into the classroom.

Suggest that children work in pairs to research one of the dinosaurs on the list. Engage them in a discussion of how to represent the length of each dinosaur. One suggestion might be to represent the length with tagboard strips. In this case, each pair of children will need tagboard strips, a ruler or measuring tape, and adhesive tape. Each inch of the tagboard strips will represent one foot of dinosaur length. The dinosaur lengths may range from about 7 feet to 70 feet, so the corresponding strips will range from 7 inches to 70 inches (almost 2 yards).

Collect and Organize Data

Have children discuss where they can find the information they need: Will you look in encyclopedias, textbooks, on the Internet? As pairs of children complete their research and construct their tagboard strips, suggest they label each strip with the name of the dinosaur and its length. Be sure all children use the same units of measurement.

Make and Interpret the Graph

Help children decide how to display the data: Could you place your strip next to the type of dinosaur listed on the board? Guide children in arranging the strips of tagboard horizontally with the longest dinosaurs on the bottom and the shortest on the top. Then have them make a strip to represent the length of the classroom. Remind them that one inch represents one foot. Then ask: Which of the dinosaurs are longer than the classroom? Which dinosaurs are shorter? Were your predictions correct?

Content Connections

NUMBERS TO 1,000

Are any of the dinosaurs listed in the graph more than 50 feet long? more than 100 feet long?

How long is the longest dinosaur in the graph? the shortest dinosaur?

Week 28: How Much is 1,000?

INVESTIGATE I have five containers and some items to put into them. Do you think 1,000 pieces of any of these items will fit into any of these containers? How can you find out?

Can It Hold 1,000?

	cotton balls	paper clips	popcorn	rice	beans
box	no	yes	yes	yes	no
milk carton	no	no	yes	no	no
half cup	no	no	no	yes	no
film cannister	no	no	no	yes	no
thimble	no	no	no	no	no

Discuss and Predict

For this investigation, you should have on hand several containers, such as a film canister, a half-cup measuring cup, a thimble, a half-pint milk container, and a gift box. You will also need several items that could be used to fill the containers, such as dried beans, unpopped popcorn, paper clips, and uncooked rice or pasta pieces.

Help children find an efficient method of counting a large number of pieces: Will you fill the container with one of these things and then count how many pieces you used? Will you make your work simpler by putting the items into groups of 10 and then into groups of 100? Would it be easier to fill the container, pour out the pieces, and then count them?

You may want to suggest that children work in teams, with each team choosing one container and one item. Have each team predict whether less than or more than 1,000 pieces of the item they chose will fit into the container.

Collect and Organize Data

Guide children in deciding how they will record their data: Will you record both the name of the container and the items you used? Will you record the total number of pieces that fit into the container? Will you compare the total to 1,000? As children count the pieces, help those who have not grouped them into tens to understand why grouping is helpful.

Make and Interpret the Table

Guide children in using the pocket graph to display their data. To display the relationships among the containers and their contents, children might use the graph pockets to make a table. After the table is complete, ask: Did 1,000 pieces fit into any of the containers? Was your prediction correct?

Content Connections

PLACE VALUE
What can the gift box hold 1,000 of?
How many gift boxes would you need to hold 1,000 cotton balls?

GI28   Graphing Investigations

Week 29: Letters in the Sentence

INVESTIGATE What makes a story easy or hard to read? Could it be the length of the sentences? Could you count the number of letters in sentences to find out?

DISCUSS AND PREDICT

Have children decide which stories they would like to investigate. You may want to have children review the books in the classroom library and then sort them by whether they are easy or hard to read. Then have children predict whether the number of letters in sentences makes a difference.

Letters in a Sentence (graph with bins: 1–10, 11–20, 21–30, 31–40, 41–50, 51–60, 61–70, 71–80, 81–90, 91–100)

COLLECT AND ORGANIZE DATA

Children might randomly select sentences by shutting their eyes, opening books, and pointing. You may want each child to print his or her sentence choice neatly on a clean sheet of paper. One way to ensure the accuracy of the count is to have children draw a vertical line after every ten letters. When they have finished grouping the letters, children can skip-count to find the total number of letters. You may want to display children's work when it is finished.

MAKE AND INTERPRET THE GRAPH

Help children decide how they will graph the data. They might want to make two graphs, one for the numbers in easy-to-read books, and one for the hard-to-read books. Then they use the graph to make generalizations about each. After the graphs are complete, ask: Which story seems to have the longer sentences and which seems to have the shorter sentences? Is this what you predicted?

Content Connections

ADDING AND SUBTRACTING

What is the difference between the number of letters in the longest sentence and the number of letters in the shortest sentence?

What is the total number of letters counted in the easy-to-read story? In the more difficult story?

Graphing Investigations GI29

A Week of Walks

INVESTIGATE How far is it from our classroom door to the swings? To the office? To the cafeteria? To the library? How do these distances compare?

Distance from Door in Paces								
swings	■	■	■	■	■	■	■	
office	■	■						
cafeteria	■		■	■				
library	■	■	■					
	0–9	10–19	20–29	30–39	40–49	50–59	60–69	70–79

Discuss and Predict

Lead children in a discussion of the distances that they would like to measure and compare on the school campus. Help them plan how they might measure the distances: Would you count paces or use a ruler? Then have children estimate and compare distances in their unit of choice. For example, you might ask which location they think is the farthest away and how many paces away it might be.

Collect and Organize Data

Children might work in groups with one child as a measurer and one as a recorder. If a distance is great, such as from the classroom door to the swings, children might break down the measurement into parts: 5 paces to the outside door, 15 paces from the door to the tree, 12 paces from the tree to the swings.

Make and Interpret the Graph

Help children decide on a scale for the graph based on the greatest distance. After the graph is complete, have children name each distance. Ask: Which distance was the longest? Which distance was the shortest? Are these the distances you predicted?

Content Connections

MULTIPLICATION AND DIVISION

Was any destination exactly a multiple of ten? How can you tell?

How many steps would it take you to go halfway to the library?

How many steps would it take to go to and from the cafeteria?

Name _____

Organizer for sorting, counting, and recording

Name _____

GI32 Graphing Investigations   Organizer for data collecting and graphing